To everything there is a season
and a time to every purpose
under the heaven:
a time to be born and a time to die;
a time to plant and a time to pluck up
that which is planted;
a time to weep and a time to laugh;
a time to mourn and a time to dance…

Eccl. 3:1, 2, 4

Salesian Missions wishes to extend special thanks and gratitude to our
generous poet friends and to the publishers who have given us permission to
reprint material included in this book. Every effort has been made to give
proper acknowledgments. Any omissions or errors are deeply regretted, and
the publisher, upon notification, will be pleased to make the necessary
corrections in subsequent editions.

First Edition Printed in the U.S.A. by Concord Litho Co., Inc., Concord,
New Hampshire 03301-0464

Seasons of the Heart

from the
Salesian Collection

Compiled and edited by
Sara Tarascio

Illustrated by
Paul Scully
Frank Massa
and Russell Bushée

Contents

Budding branch, greening sod,
Robin's song praising God.
Every leaf, every note,
Waking life, lifting hope.

Minnie Boyd Popish

I Have No Need of Fancy Things

I have no need of fancy things
like diamonds and gold,
For I'm content with simple things
as autumn leaves unfold.

Blessings daily come my way
with loved ones by my side
Upon the carousel of life
with Jesus as my Guide.

I'm comforted when things go wrong
in seasons of distress
By simple words like, "I love you!"
that bring such happiness.

I walk in awe beside the sea
in the twilight's purple haze
And contemplate the stars above
with heartfelt, silent praise.

I watch the seasons come and go,
summer green to autumn gold...
I have no need of fancy things
with simple treasures to behold!

Clay Harrison

Gifts of the Heart

Gifts of the heart are a cavalcade
Of treasures that will never fade;
Like the look in a special someone's eyes -
That lifts your soul up to the skies -

Like a dazzling sunrise that greets the day,
Awash in a rainbow and dewdrop display;
Like maple leaves full of Autumn's fire -
And Winter's sparkled white attire -

Like Spring-dressed trees and blooming flowers
And purple lilac covered bowers,
Gifts of the heart are glorious and grand -
And bestowed to us by the Master's hand.

Nora M. Bozeman

He's My Friend

I wake to God each morning
In the light of early dawn.
As I go from chore to chore,
He's the strength I draw upon.

If I falter in the middle
Of an overwhelming task,
I can feel Him lift the load
A bit - I never have to ask.

If frustration overwhelms me
Or my confidence departs,
I feel His love inside me
And His hand upon my heart.

If sorrow overcomes me
Or my mind is in despair,
If my body's sore afflicted,
I just pray - He's always there.

I thank Him for the joys I've found
For all the folks who love me,
For beauty I see all around
And in the skies above me.

It matters not the burden
Or what events betide me,
So long as God will hold my hand
And always walk beside me.

Betty Stewart-Fuller

Lighter Than Air

My simple wish
Is peace in my mind,
Love in my heart
That others will find.

The sun on my face
A breeze at my back,
And of God's blessings,
All of those that I lack.

My He show favor
And come unto me,
And make my lifetime
All that it should be.

And last of all, Lord
A good friend around,
To lighten my spirits
When I am down.

Nothing material, Lord,
Just that you can spare
The things that I pray for
That are lighter than air.

James Joseph Huesgen

Sunset Years

When in the Sunset Years of life
My friend - be not afraid
'Tis then the glory of His face
Will soon to you be made!

Even though youth's past and strength be gone
So, too, be beauty lost
The price is paid for suffering's lot
Just memory knows the bitter cost!

Oh, the bliss of heaven's kiss
On cheeks stained with life's tears
Whate'er your lot - God's not forgot
Those many helpless fears.

Great the reward for those who wait
God's "Sacred Spot" to stand
And oh the joy - when all are One -
Held in His loving Hand!

Kathryn Wiesenhoefer

...Take courage and be strong.
Fear not and be not dismayed,
because the Lord thy God is with thee
wherever thou shalt go.
Joshua 1:9

God Is Good

The Lord has cast His majesty
Upon the land - the sky and sea -
And we are privileged to see
The wonders He has made to be,
But He has also graced with mirth
Some gifts He sowed upon the earth
To add to joys and smiles of life
And be, forever, ours - and rife.

No matter where we choose to go,
We see what He has made or sowed -
From rolling hills to grassy plains;
Trees and plants of green and flame;

And mountain crags that touch the sky -
As if to challenge and defy
The glories He has sown below,
Where rivers flow and lilies grow.

All gifts, so wondrous and grand,
He willed to sky - the sea and land -
That is our privilege to share
And keep, forever, in our care;
All gifts of God to light our ways
And add to joys of night and day -
And be reminders of the truth
That God is love - and heart of ruth.

Michael Dubina

13

Blessings

I waited for the sunshine,
the clouds were dark and gray,
Prayed that God would hear me
and cast me not away.
It seemed as if forever
I cried to Him in vain,
Then it happened oh so quickly,
came the best and greatest change.
It wasn't what I asked for
in my selfish soul-torn way,
But much better than I hoped for
all my fears He did allay.
So my friend do not be anxious,
He will answer in His time
And send blessings by the millions,
You alone could never find.

Kathryn Wiesenhoefer

You Can Be a Sunbeam

You can be a ray of sunshine
Where there is adversity,
For your light can be the spark
That ignites humanity.
Simple words of consolation
Can relinquish fear or sorrow,
And the warmth your love exudes
Will be the joy of each tomorrow.
For caring is a virtue
That somehow illuminates
And spreads to form an aura
With the glow that it creates.
And those who render tenderness
Are like the sun's reflections,
That warm and spread their radiance
Throughout the world in all directions.

The sharing of your bounty
With those less fortunate than you,
Is the key that channels love and hope
To bring the sun in view.
For God enriched your life with much
Not to keep... but to expand,
By joining other sunbeams
To bring His light unto the land.
You can be that ray of sunshine
To keep God's love-lamp burning
And the power of your one small light
Will light the world, 'til His returning.

Patience Allison Hartbauer

15

The Open Door

Dear Jesus knocking at my door
Please let me open wide,
The door that I have locked within,
So You can come inside.

The hinges are corroded
For I've kept it shut too long.
I hope now that it's open
You'll find little there that's wrong.

For while I stayed in darkness
And refused the sunlight in,
I was bound to lose direction
And fall deeply into sin.

But I've finally pried it open
And I feel Your presence there.
My heart is filled with sunlight
And the smell of clean, fresh air.

The birds above are singing
And my heart is singing, too,
Because I've swung wide open
The door that's meant for You.

Grace Grisafe

The Heavens Declare His Handiwork

Radiant beams of sunlight
touch morning's fresh dewdrop,
glorious bursts of color
on flowering mountaintop,
fragile little blade of grass
beneath the strong oak tree,
are samples of God's handiwork
declared for all to see.

Raindrops are splashing earthward
from skies of barren gray,
muddy rivulets in corn fields
replenish rivers far away,
amidst thunder, lightning flashing
illuminates the land,
while even the blackest night
affirms the Master's hand.

Outpouring of the Son-Light,
blessings descend like rain,
heaven declares God's glory,
again, and yet again,
Omnipotent Father,
Blessed Jesus, Holy Ghost,
dipping deeply in His storehouse,
giving us His uttermost.

Dorothea K. Barwick

*The heavens declare
the glory of God;
and the firmament sheweth
His handiwork.*
Ps. 19:1

17

Your Faith

Your faith must be the keystone
Of all you ever do,
For if that faith is lacking
Your life is wanting too.

Your faith must be most constant
And steadfast day by day,
For if that faith should waver
You well may lose your way.

Your faith will guide and lead you
And be your shining light.
Faith that is true and lasting
Will make your life more bright.

Harold F. Mohn

There Are No Endings

This I have found among the twisted ways,
The narrow paths converging into one,
Somewhere beyond the setting of the sun,
When dusk lends softness to the web of days,
And weary hours sink to blend among
The quiet peace, where a silver star
Reminds me Heaven isn't all that far,
Whose ladder hope has fashioned, rung by rung.
Where reason seeks the meaning of a man,
Hearts can sense the things eyes cannot see,
Though life remains the greatest mystery,
Love holds the clue within a gentle hand.
"There are no endings, only pauses when
We look for new beginnings once again."

Grace E. Easley

Within...
a Song

With nature all around me,
Such gives my soul a lift,
Along each trail and pathway
I find such lovely gifts.

There are friends to warm me
as I stumble along the way,
Their warmth, and care, and giving
Brighten my every day.

There are sweet moods that fill me,
How this life doth here impart,
But I find no thing more winsome,
Than this song within my heart.

Ah... 'Tis a life of what we make it
And if yours is less than true,
Come with me sister and brother
Let me share a bit with you.

James Joseph Huesgen

*Sing
to the Lord
a new song,
his praise is from
the ends of
the earth...*
Is. 42:10

A Matter of
the Heart

It's often been suggested
that faith is truly blind,
For those who don't possess it
can't see it in their mind.
Because they have not seen it,
they say it can't exist,
For never have they felt it
the scholars all insist.

Have they never seen a rainbow
and marveled at such art?
Have they never known the Artist
who dwells within the heart?
Have they never seen the forest
change from green to gold,
Or wondered at the snowflakes
as winter days unfold?

Have they never seen the miracle
of a mother giving birth,
Or felt their hearts strangely warmed
by wonders beyond earth?
The things of earth bear witness
to nobler things above,
For it's a matter of the heart
that reveals the Father's love!

Clay Harrison

*...blessed are they
that have not seen,
and have believed.*
John 20:29

21

Tides

Life - a tide, with an ebb and a flow,
tossing you high, smashing you low.
Sometimes you ride on the crest of the wave;
Sometimes - in the pit of a bottomless cave.
But a tide has a way of running its course;
wiser, perhaps, is to look for the source.
Is the flow from an outgoing, generous fount,
surging and swelling, snags to surmount;
or does it recede, with a shy weather-eye,
waiting for some secret sign from the sky;
afraid of a whirl, never making a splash,
aiming short of the crest for fear of the crash,

and content to be tossed without purpose or goal,
running aground on an uncharted shoal?
I hope that life's more than a coming and going,
more than a storm-battered undertowing -
only touching the shoreline and never the shore.
Surely life is a promise, not mystic lore:
a chance to aim and to reach for the sun,
gaining strength from trials tenaciously won;
holding a towline to others "at sea,"
adrift in the tide of humanity.

Barbara A. McDowell

Life
Today

Dreams in shambles, strewn at my feet.
Pictures drawn, but not complete.
Hope is there, in all her glory.
To help me live, and finish my story.

Trudge along, this road of life.
Smile and laugh, in the face of strife.
The task is hard, facing pain.
But in order to grow, all things need rain.

The ache grows, soul filled with sorrow.
I must live today, never tomorrow.
Embracing chaos, swirling about.
Standing fast, choking the shout.

The Armor of God, buckled tight.
Firm in faith, all things right.

James Monroe Munyon V

God's
Gifts

I do not ask for jewels,
for I have eyes that see
the moon, the stars, the flowers,
the growing of a tree.

I do not ask for riches,
for I have ears that hear
the wind, the sea, the music,
the voice of people dear.

I do not ask for power,
for I have lips that speak
of God and love and kindness,
of things all men should seek.

For I'm the Lord's own child,
there's nothing that I lack
and of the gifts He's given me,
He does not want them back.

Eleanor M. Torchia

Homeless

Alone in the world, with no one to care,
Or to help if their lives go awry.
They stumble through life, one day at a time,
While the rest of the world passes by.

They forage for food and clothing and such,
In the back streets and alleys of town.
When their body is tired they have no place to go,
They must look for a place to lie down.

In this great land of ours, with all of its wealth,
It saddens my heart just to see,
There are so many hungry and homeless lost lives
And except for God's grace - there go we.

So tonight when you finish your lovely big meal
And retire to your warm comfy bed,
Say a prayer for all those who have nothing to eat
Or no place to lay their poor head.

Evelene E. Henrion

...Amen
I say to you, as long as
you did it to one of these,
my least brethren,
you did it to me.
Matt. 25:40

For the Blessings of the Year

For each beauty that I know,
For the gifts Thou dost bestow:
Clothing, home, and family dear,
For my friends both far and near;
Thank You, Lord, You giveth me
Every blessing full and free.

Thank You, Lord, for snows that fall,
Summer rains, and birds that call;
Thank You, Lord, for food we eat;
Fruit and grain; and seasons sweet.
Thank You, Lord, You marked by hand
Every bounty of the land.

Thank You, Lord, for healing sure,
Goodly moments, calm and pure;
For Thy guidance, peace and cheer,
For each blessing of the year...
Lord, these words I lift to Thee
Knowing well Thou lovest me.

Roxie Lusk Smith

*"Thanks
be to God
for His
inexpressible
gift!"*
2 Cor. 9:15

*A*nd all these blessings
shall come upon you
and overtake you,
if you hear His voice.

Deut. 28:2

What More Proof

I've watched the petals of a rose
Unfold to greet the day.
I've seen bright tulips opening
To catch the sunbeam's ray.
I've seen the golden daffodils
Emerge from frozen sod
To grace the springtime fields and hills...
Still, some say there's no God.

I've seen the painted autumn leaves,
The flaming countryside.
I've strolled through winding rustic lanes
Where peace and charm abide.
I've seen the yellow sunflowers
Give folk a cheerful nod
That lightened hearts who passed their way...
Still, some say there's no God.

I've watched the crimson sunset's glow,
The mountains' majesty.
I've seen a brilliant redbird perch
Upon a snow-clad tree.
And still some doubt. I know they must
Not see the things I see.
Each day is filled with miracles.
What more proof need there be?

Beverly J. Anderson

They Led Me in God's Way

I must go home again,
Back to the old home place,
Where yesterdays still live,
Back to the old home base.

'Twas there that I was born
And there that I was raised
In family atmosphere
That truly was love-laced.

'Twas there I learned to pray,
To say my table grace,
To love my fellowman
And always give God praise.

I must go home again,
Back to the old home place,
To Mother and to Dad
Who led me in God's way.

Loise Pinkerton Fritz

Hearken unto thy father
that begat thee, and despise
not thy mother when she is old.
Proverbs 23:22

God's Love Is All Around Us!

God's love is all around us
and beautiful it is to see,
Like Autumn leaves a'falling
and the rippling of the sea,
Like flowers in full bloom
with colors glowing bright,
Like fireflies all around us
just lighting up the night.
God's love is in a rainbow
shining in the sky
And with the little birds
that are ever flying nigh,
In our little children,
precious one and all,
In Winter and the Springtime,
the Summer and the Fall.
God's love is on the mountain
where the trees are very green
And down in the valley
where much of life is seen.
In a time of sorrow
surely it is found,
When all your friends and loved ones
are come to gather round.
God's love is not just things
that we can see or own,
It's also what's inside us
to help to take us home...

Kaye Deal Penley

31

The Quaint Old Chapel

There's a quaint old chapel that I love;
it's perched beside the sea,
and often do I meditate
within its walls, consolingly.

From out the window, far and wide,
the tides both come and go;
the music of the chanting waves,
the most soothing that I know.

No care withstands the tranquil sound
that puts the soul at ease
and to the sorrows I may know,
brings full and sweet release

That when I leave I've been made new;
a gift straight from the sea,
which makes the quaint old chapel
a very special place for me.

Don Beckman

Regrets

I regret the times and moments
That I've made another cry:
Times of anger, trial or struggle,
When I argued or defied;
I regret the trusts I've broken
In some hours of despair
When - for selfish greeds or reasons -
I was sinful or unfair;
And I rue the lies I've spoken
To my friends (and in my prayers)
That were meant to gain me favors
Of content, or holy care;
But I'm, mostly, sad and sorry
For the agonies and tears
I have made the Lord to suffer
In my sinful-wayward years.

Michael Dubina

Blessings From God

As I sit and rest each day
And watch the Summer fade away
I see the birds as they fly by
The fleecy clouds up in the sky.

I watch the leaves as they turn red,
Then brown and yellow as they shed,
But God preserves these trees to bear
A brand-new crop in fresh Spring air.

The birds return each year and nest
And raise their families in its crest.
He sees that flowers bloom in Spring
With fragrant scents such joy they bring.

All of His blessings are so grand,
Because of our Lord's loving hands.
So say a prayer to Him each night
For all these wondrous sights so bright.

Albert N. Theel

Thoughts of Thankfulness

For happy times of joy and mirth,
for harvest riches from the earth,
for challenges that test our worth -
we thank You, Lord, for all of these.

For nursery songs a mother sings,
for fireflies and bluebirds' wings,
for all life's gentle, little things -
we thank You, Lord, for such as these.

For peace that sheathes the warrior's sword,
for noble deed and kindly word,
for lands where freedom's voice is heard -
we thank You, Lord, grant these increase!

For home and hearth where we can rest
among the dear ones we know best,
for all good things whereby we're blessed -
we thank You, Lord, for gifts like these.

For every church and holy place
where we may come to seek Your grace
and know that no one's rank or race
will cause Your love for us to cease.

We thank You, Lord, and pray that we
may closer grow in harmony
till goodwill clothes humanity
in robes of brotherhood and peace!

John C. Bonser

Someone

There always is Someone who cares
And bears a love for you,
Someone unseen but near your side
In all you ever do...
Someone to comfort and console
Your sorrow and despair,
Someone to give you strength and hope
And help your burdens share...
Someone to turn to in distress
When all seems lost and vain,
Someone to bring you confidence,
Your long sought goal to gain...
Who is this Someone you may ask
Who shows such care and love,
Beyond the shadow of a doubt
It's God, the Lord above.

Harold F. Mohn

A Wondrous Dream

I dreamed a wondrous dream last night,
Too wondrous to be true,
For none of gray clouds were in sight
And skies were bright and blue.

A glorious sun was shining down
Upon an earth serene
And smiles had chased away a frown,
Oh, what a wondrous scene!

Last night I dreamed a dream of peace,
Of "peace on earth, good will t'ward men";
Where striving souls had found release
Within our Savior's love again!

Clayton G. Moseley

Love

When Jesus trod the paths of earth
He must have loved so much
The hills, the trees, the flowers, the grass,
For oft' He spoke of such.

He must have loved to gaze above
As eve was drawing nigh,
When clouds that changed to red and gold
Made beautiful the sky.

He also must have loved to see
The children at their play,
And when they had their little hurts,
To wipe the tears away.

But so much more than all of these,
He loved us, everyone,
And gave His life that we might live,
For He was God's own Son.

Rachel Hartnett

*For God
so loved the world
that He gave His only begotten,
that whosoever believeth in Him
should not perish, but have
everlasting life.*
John 3:16

God's
Sweet Release

I find my peace in the pathless woods
Or by some deserted shore,
Along a winding country road
Where I've never been before.

To walk knee-deep in a daisy field
As I did long years ago,
And hear the song the robin sings
These things, I love and know.

The singing wind in whispering pines
When dusk is cathedral dim,
And then to God, for this sweet release,
My grateful thanks to Him.

Gene Appleby

Amazing

Isn't it amazing that tears and rain alike
Can cleanse the stain that living brings,
and leave all fresh and bright.

Isn't it amazing that a Savior from above
Came to earth to save our souls,
Because of holy love.

Isn't it amazing that each is given free,
The tears, the rain, the saving grace -
God gave them all to me.

Gael Phaneuf

"...it is by grace you have been saved."
Ephesians 2:5

40

Prayer of the Aging

Here I am again, O Lord,
Alone and old and needing,
Praying for help again, O Lord,
Please listen to my pleading.
For all the times I've hurt You,
When only You could know,
Forgive my sinful, erring soul
And make it white as snow.
I know You hear my every prayer
No matter what I seek.
Today I pray again, O Lord,
For this body, tired and weak.
Even though I'm growing old,
Heal and make me strong.
And if it be Your loving will
I'll live a life that's long.
I pray for friends and family
Watch over them each day,
For suffering children everywhere,
Take their pain away.
I also pray for all the sick
The imprisoned and the oppressed,
For all those who will die this day,
A place of eternal rest.
I pray for a world so troubled by
Hunger, drugs and wars,
You alone can stop these Lord,
The power is only Yours.
Thank You, Lord, for listening
And for our daily needs
I'll pray again tomorrow -
Be with me, O Lord, please.

R. Zielinski

I Am Learning, Lord

My life has taken many falls
and tumbles 'long the way.
The many trials have left me
in a sure state of dismay,
For with each trial, I tried alone
to tend, and soothe, and mend,
Instead of giving them to God -
and on Him just depend...

But I am learning, Lord.

It seems I was determined
to carry all the load;
I longed for smoother pathways,
yet I walked a rocky road.
Little did I understand -
God waited patiently
To pave a new beginning
with a better life for me...

But I am learning, Lord.

It took a real disaster
to bring me to my knees;
To finally call upon the Lord,
and say, "God help me please."
He came with no delaying,
with strong arms that would hold -
The weight of all my burdens;
He gladly took the load...

And I am learning, Lord.

What a needless cross I carried,
all because I could not see -
What a friend I have in Jesus,
and the love He has for me.
Peace I find when troubles hover,
tho' the outcome is unknown,
For if yet the road is rocky,
I won't walk it all alone...

For I am learning, Lord.

Diana Sue Helmer

$\mathcal{O}$h, how dark life seems sometimes,
there seems to be no hope
for brighter days as we have seen,
we feel we just can't cope.
But amid those dark and dreary days
a light somehow shines through
and I hear a voice so soft and sweet
say "I'm hear to strengthen you.
I have been right here by your side through
all your toils and tears,
I've seen your hardship, felt your pain
and yearned to ease your fears...
Oh, child of Mine rest assured of My great
love for you...
As I reach out to take your hand -
reach out to take Mine too...
Let Me be your source of strength,
your guide unto the end
for like no other love you've known
you have no greater Friend...
Behold My presence, feel My love,
see... I care for you
and look up child for I am here to
love and strengthen you!"

Beverly Huff

44

Contrasts

Life is filled with many contrasts
Winter - Summer, Spring or Fall.
Darkness always ends in dawning,
Weary moments come to all.
Sometime showers - sometimes shadows
Yet again the sun shines through,
Moments may be sweet or bitter
Dark clouds change to skies of blue.

Trials and blessings - gladness - sorrow
Each a portion of our life,
Yesterdays - each new tomorrow
Happiness along with strife.
Nature's beauties, soft in Springtime
Golden Summers - shining bright,
Autumn brings breathtaking beauty
Snowflakes dance on Winter's night.

Miracles - a touch of magic,
Sometimes laughter - sometimes tears,
Rainbows when the storm is over,
Faith - believing - joys and fears.
Words of wisdom - words in anger,
Portion take - a portion give,
Promise of a bright tomorrow
Contrasts in this life we live.

Garnett Ann Schultz

Little Bird

One little bird
In a bare tree,
One little snowbird,
No more can I see.
Puffed up with the cold,
Alone and forlorn,
I wonder what sorrows
The wee thing has borne.
I hope that the sun
His wings will soon warm
And the blast of the winds
Will do him no harm.
Let us scatter out crumbs
That, at least, he may eat
And stop for a moment
A prayer to repeat
That God in His love
For all creatures will send
A feathered companion
To be his staunch friend.

Minnie Boyd Popish

Whatever
Your Cross

Whatever your cross, whatever your pain,
There will always be sunshine after the rain.
Perhaps you may stumble, perhaps even fall,
But God's always ready to answer your call.

He knows every heartache, sees every tear -
A word from His lips can calm every fear.
Your sorrows may linger throughout the night
But suddenly vanish at dawn's early light.

The Savior is waiting somewhere above
To give you His grace and send you His love.
Whatever your cross, whatever your pain,
God always sends rainbows after the rain.

Clay Harrison

In Us He Abides

When tears wet the pillow
And dark is the night,
When family forsakes you
And friends, too, take flight...
When burdens are heavy
And cares press the soul,
Then look to the Saviour,
He cares for His own.

When dark seems the pathway
And hope's at low ebb,
Then turn to the Saviour,
Recall what He said:
"I'll never forsake you,"
In us He abides;
In shadow or sunlight
He's there as our Guide.

Loise Pinkerton Fritz

*And he that keepeth
His commandments
dwelleth in Him, and He in him.
And hereby we know that He abideth in us,
by the Spirit which He hath given us.*
I John 3:24

When God Is Silent

When life's obstacles and trials
Seem like bars across our way,
Keeping us from moving onward,
We must rest and wait and pray.

But when time shows us no changes,
Our faith wavers and grows dim -
Yet it's here hope strengthens, as we
Cast our helplessness on Him.

In our darkness hope gives courage
Helping us to calmly wait,
Giving us the blest assurance
God will soon unlatch the gate.

When God's silent, there's a reason,
Tho' we do not understand,
God is working in the silence
For our good with purpose grand.

So, we'll wait and trust God's wisdom,
Tho' these walls still can't be moved,
For it's in this very spot, friend,
Where God's power shall be proved!

Beverly J. Anderson

...Blessed
are all they
who put their trust
in Him.
Ps. 2:12

$\mathcal{W}$ithin the withered, barren earth
in winter, waits the violet's birth;
Beneath brown slopes, white-flecked with snow,
a field of daisies starts to grow.
Deep in our own thorn-threatened lives
each seedling soul, undaunted, thrives
Till on time's sheer and sightless wall,
where nothing seems to cling at all,
Some weak yet valiant vines disclose
the coming triumph of the rose!

John C. Bonser

God's Magnificence

We are explorers more or less,
In life's uncharted wilderness,
So much remains for those to find,
Who have an open, eager mind.
A miracle beyond belief,
The fragile texture of a leaf,
No laboratory can produce
A snow-capped mountain green with spruce.

No chemist's beaker can contain,
The crystal formula for rain,
You will not find a patent on
The coral ribbons of the dawn.
Say what you will, nobody knows
What truly makes a living rose,
In spite of all we've learned so far,
Man cannot duplicate a star.

The cool grey moss, the ivied vine,
Aren't rolled from an assembly line,
The palette of the artist holds
No match for Autumn's reds and golds.
The greatest sonnet ever penned,
Is but an echo of the wind,
And all things past and all things hence,
...Attest to God's Magnificence.

Grace E. Easley

A Blossom
Uncovered

Like a blossom just discovered
amid dry and barren ground -
loveliness uncovered,
a splendor that was found.

So, too, may we have seeds
of beauty deep within
that are covered by the weeds
of adversities and sin.

We have a way to break through
the barrenness we face;
God provided us an avenue
of abundance through His grace.

We need only to come humbly
to the new life through His Son
to blossom forth more beautifully
than we have ever done.

Barbara A. McDowell

*Those who trust
in the Lord are as Mt. Zion...
and will endure forever.*
Ps. 125:1

Pause
a Moment

Pause a moment in your day
Speak to God and softly pray,
Matters not where you might be
'Neath a lovely Springtime tree,
Maybe in the forest deep
With all nature fast asleep.

Pause a moment on the lane
Walking in the April rain,
Look for blue skies high above
'Neath a rainbow that you love,
Kneel upon the warming sod
Take the time to talk to God.

Cast your every care aside
In your Maker then confide,
All your hurts and all your fears
Wipe away the bitter tears,
Reach - you'll surely touch a star
Pause a moment where you are.

Garnett Ann Schultz

For You, O Lord,
have delivered my soul
from death, my eyes from tears,
my feet from stumbling.
Ps. 116:8

53

Growing
Closer

I feel us growing closer,
Than we ever were before,
The shadows that I cringed from,
Don't haunt me anymore.
Your Presence fills the room until
I half expect to see
You standing here beside my bed,
and looking down at me.

I'm not afraid of getting lost,
Because at last I know
You love me far too deeply,
To ever let me go.
You stand between the world and me,
Defender of my soul,
Until at last, eternity
Is mine to have and hold.

I'm seeing for the first time,
All I could not, before.
You fill each waking hour,
With blessed peace, and more.
You have replaced my old self,
With a new one You designed,
And now You are the only love,
Within this life of mine.

I feel us growing closer,
And my heart is glad, because
Never once did You forsake me,
With my failings and my flaws.
But instead, You held me gently,
As I told my tale of woe,
And I whispered, "Master love me,
...And never let me go!"

Grace E. Easley

When Kindness
Comes A-Knockin'

When kindness comes a-knockin'
Share the love He has bestowed -
When another has a burden
Help carry the heavy load.

When kindness comes a-knockin'
And thankfulness fills the air,
Speak words of gratitude to others
Show them how much you care.

When kindness comes a-knockin'
Find the time to send
That letter of encouragement
To a downcast friend.

For kindness is that special ingredient -
Oft called an "added touch,"
So sprinkle the world with kindness
'Cause it's a recipe folks love so much!

So when kindness comes a-knockin'
Open the door of your heart wide,
For being kind is catchy
And will perk you up inside!

Linda C. Grazulis

Make Someone Happy

Make someone happy. You can, you know.
It doesn't take much for a heart to glow.
It doesn't take much for a spark to fire,
Just a gentle breath and a firm desire.

A letter written from the heart,
Filled with words that care, will... a fire, start
Deep inside a one who so needs a blaze.
Blow gently then, with a word of praise,

With a word of joy that may cause a smile
As the words are read. Ah, it's so worthwhile.
Take the time to hear on the telephone,
Someone needs to talk, listen to the tone.

Listen to the mood, take the time to hear,
Ah, a friend who cares is so dear, so dear.
Make someone happy. You can, you know.
It doesn't take much for a heart to glow.

Dolores Dahl

Prayer
for Fishermen

For all the fishermen on earth
I say this prayer today,
Be generous to them, O Lord
And help them on their way.
As once You talked to Peter and
He cast his humble net,
So may their daily catch become
As great as it can get.
But also in my prayer I ask
This miracle again,
That they not only search the sea
But try to fish for men.
To fish for souls to do Your will
And spread Your gospel true,
As Your disciples on this earth
To praise and honor You.
I pray that every fisherman
Wherever he may be
Will turn his thoughts to You and to
The Sea of Galilee.

James J. Metcalfe

God Will Supply Your Need

Are you wandering through life
In total despair,
Searching for peace
And freedom from care?
The answer is Jesus -
He's calling today;
Your sins He can pardon
Your soul He can save.
He promises all of your need
He will meet,
For His grace is sufficient,
His pardon complete.
Just put faith in Him and His strength,
Not your own,
And He'll wash your heart clean,
Take your sins to atone.
Then, with peace in your heart,
Where the Savior abides,
With great joy you can say,
"All my need He supplies!"

Shirley W. Langley

*But my God
shall supply all your need
according to His riches
in Glory by Christ Jesus.*
Phil. 4:19

59

What
Is Spring?

Spring is the time when crocus grow,
When Winter winds no longer blow;
When we can hear the songs of birds,
As other Springtime sounds are heard.

Spring is the time of hopefulness,
When hearts lift up for love's caress;
When budding trees are on display,
And fragrant flowers in sweet array.

Spring is the time, once long ago,
When Christ, through death, defeated foe;
And then arose from out of tomb,
As wiped away were tears of gloom!

Sancie Earman King

Disciple of God

I want to have a closer walk
With You, my Lord, today;
I want to feel Your tender touch
In everything, I pray.

I want this joy that others seek
To reach another plane;
Uplift me from these worldly cares
Pour out Your Spirit again.

I thirst, my Lord, from day to day,
Please quench me, as You fill
My soul to overflowing, God.
In faith, I know You will.

Now, make me usable, my Lord,
To spread Your Holy Word,
And reach into some dormant hearts
In case they have not heard.

Then they will know the joy I feel
From closer walks with Thee.
You are the Way, the Truth, the Life
for all Eternity!

Gene Appleby

Wondrous
Beauty

Spring arrived in wondrous beauty,
Out my window I can see
Daffodils in all their glory,
Buds adorning every tree.

And I pause in awe and wonder,
Then I thank the Lord above,
For He kindly gives these treasures
Unconditionally with love.

Thank You so, most gracious Father
For Spring's loveliest of days
And all things of nature's wonder
That You send along the way.

Thank You for renewed assurance,
Springtime's own sweet gentle song,
Flowers that show their face of beauty
While birds sweetly sing along.

And with Spring's sweet sound of beauty
Earthly changes now take place,
Thank You for the showers of blessings
All in sweet amazing grace.

Katherine Smith Matheney

Giving
Thanks

Thank You, God, for the flowers,
Sunny days and ivy bowers,
Rainbows bright and moonlit nights,
Mountain peaks and lofty sights.
Thank You, God, for honey bees,
Bobolinks and April's breeze,
Backwood lanes and babbling brooks,
Woodlands dense and sheltered nooks.
Thank You, God, for all good things,
The bird upon the eave that sings,
The happy sound of tots at play,
Azure skies on summer's day.
Thank You, God, for home and kin,
Harvest and a well-stocked bin,
A springtime rain, a garden rose,
And twilight's aura at day's close.

Virginia Borman Grimmer

Give thanks
to the Lord,
call upon His name,
make known
His deeds...
    1 Chr. 16:8

The Little Things of Life

We speak of life in terms of age,
of time and death and space,
as we too often speak of men
in terms of creeds and race;
and yet how many times our dreams
which soar on silver wings
are built around the day to day
events - life's "little things!"

Our street that's not just any street,
the house in which we live;
the duties of the job we hold,
the gifts we get - and give.
The friends we like despite their faults,
the neighbors 'cross the way;
the laughter of our children and
the clever things they say!

For life is more than just romance
or beauty, fame and grace;
it is the cares and tears we share,
the love that lights a face;
it is our joys, our prayers, our fears,
our faith, the songs we sing,
it is the total worth of each
important "little thing!"

John C. Bonser

Just Walk
Beside Me

"Don't walk too far ahead, I may not follow."
Your steps are so much swifter than my own,
If I lose sight of you within the distance,
I doubt I can continue on alone.

"Don't walk too far behind, I may not lead."
I lack the strength of soul that you possess,
And if you lost your way because of me,
Then both of us would face a wilderness.

"But walk beside me"... so that I may know
The sweet companionship your presence brings,
So may we, hand in hand, and heart to heart,
Help each other on to higher things.

Grace E. Easley

...if we walk in the light, as He is in the light,
we have fellowship one with another, and the blood
of Jesus Christ, His Son, cleanseth us from all sin.
1 John 1:7

Time forever has barred the way
You can't return to yesterday.
Out of reach - beyond the blue -
Tomorrow waits in vain for you!
So take today, enjoy its measure
Quick as a flash - it's yesterday's treasure!

Maxine Lung

Praise the Lord!

If you can smile when your heart is broken
and laugh in sorrow's face...
If you can ignore the harsh word spoken
with humility and grace,
Praise the Lord!
If you can resist the next temptation
and rebound when you fail...
If you can sing through tribulation
and pray when fears assail,
Praise the Lord!
If you can finish the race you started
knowing the race is won...
If you can sail the course you charted
through storm and setting sun,
Praise the Lord!
If you can forgive the sins of others
who brought you pain today...
If you can respect all men as brothers
and always earn your pay,
Praise the Lord!
If you can befriend the lost and friendless
with kindness from your cup...
If you can prevail when doubts seem endless
refusing to give up,
Praise the Lord!

Clay Harrison

In everything give thanks;
for this is the will of God
in Christ Jesus for you.
1 Ths. 5:18

A Prayer
in My Garden

Thank You, Dear Lord, for the little seeds
that have sprouted and are growing here.
Thank You for all of life's precious things
and loved ones we hold so dear.

Thank You for life on this beautiful earth
with all of its hidden treasure,
Thank You for Spring and the new life it brings
with bountiful gifts beyond measure.

Thank You for love You have placed in our hearts
to scatter through family and friends,
Thank You for Jesus, Your greatest of gifts
and the promise that love never ends.

Viola Shrum Webb

Life's Road

I cannot walk life's road alone
I do not know the way,
The twists and turns confuse my mind
If I should go or stay.

But oh, I have a Friend Who knows
He's been this way before,
He is ever there to guide me
On smooth or rocky shore.

In youth I felt quite confident
And walked life's road alone
But my ego soon was shattered
By failures, all my own.

At last I found the answer
To keep forevermore;
I walk life's road with Jesus
Who passed this way before.

Kay Hoffman

Raindrops Falling

Raindrops softly falling
In a gentle melody
Refreshing plants and flowers
And soothing peacefully
The thoughts that oft' are troubled
Or racing "to and fro";
Raindrops softly falling
Seem to comfort mortal woe.

As the lovely growth of springtime
Is accomplished by the rain
May the heart grown worn and weary
Or encompassed now in pain

Find gentle sweet refreshing
In the blessedness of showers
Falling softly in sweet rhythm
To renew these hearts of ours.

God has His special blessings
As they come to everyone
Just at its needed season,
Springtime rain or summer sun,
Or the brilliant glow of autumn
And in winter's snowy white.
All are given for enjoyment
By our Living Lord of Light.

Jewell Carr Campbell

All Things
Will Fall
Into Place

When tears are shed and we question why
And it seems we find life hard to face,
Remember friend, with the help of God,
All things will fall into place.

Life at times seems hard and cruel
And we can't seem to find God's grace,
Remember friend, with the help of God,
All things will fall into place.

There are times that are tough and sometimes rough
And we make mistakes in our haste,
Remember friend, with the help of God,
All things will fall into place.

After stormy periods the sun will shine
And our sorrows will all be erased,
Remember friend, with the help of God,
All things will fall into place.

If we would just learn to let go and let God
And always make this the case,
Remember friend, with the help of God,
All things will fall into place.

Shirley Hile Powell

Fear not,
for I am with you…
I will strengthen you,
I will help you…
Is. 41:10

How Nice
It Would Be

How nice it would be
to return to the years
That were absent of worry
and absent of fears -
And full of the laughter
and joys of content
That God had created -
to never be spent.
Years of fulfillment -
of pleasures and truths -
That are His endowment
to children and youth
And there - once again -
to run through the years
That never knew heartaches
or troubles of tears.
Just years of His glories,
for youth to enjoy,
With dreams and adventures
for all girls and boys -
And a prayer of contentment,
to end every day,
For the loves and the pleasures
of living and play.

Michael Dubina

...Amen I say to you,
unless you be converted,
and become as little children,
you shall not enter
the kingdom of heaven.
Matt. 18:3

Autumn Rapture

I, when the summer was over,
Found autumn was covered with gold,
And colors more lovely than springtime
Were there for these eyes to behold.

Lost in a sweet fascination
I gazed on with wonder and awe,
Then rapt in serene adoration
Praised God in the glory I saw.

George R. Kossik

The First Sighting

The geese are flying south today,
I see them on the wing.
"We're flying to a warmer spot,"
I seem to hear them sing.
Above the autumn-frosted land
They fly so leisurely,
As one in the formation "V"
So aptly takes the lead.

The geese are on the wing today,
They all are southward bound.
Way up in God's heavens high
I hear their honking sounds.
Since winter's just around the bend,
Their message I hear ring:
"We're going to a warmer clime
But we'll return next spring."

Loise Pinkerton Fritz

While the earth remaineth,
seedtime and harvest,
and cold and heat,
and summer and winter,
and day and night
shall not cease.
Genesis 8:22

Give Me a Golden Day

Do please give me a golden day
Where sunbeams dance and breezes play,
'Neath skies of blue - in fields of green
With magic moments tucked between,
To stand atop the highest hill
Within the day all calm and still.

A golden day - a heart that's free
A winding road that beckons me,
Some cloud-boats sailing in the sky
A bumblebee - a butterfly,
Perhaps a touch of magic green
And ripples on the flowing stream.

Oh, for a glimpse of paradise
That sparkles right before my eyes,
As nature lends her magic real
To make the day, a day ideal,
With fields so fresh with new-mown hay
Dear God, give me a golden day.

Garnett Ann Schultz

Seasons of Life

The autumn leaves of red and gold
Are whirling, swirling down,
But here and there
From branches bare;
A stubborn few hang on.

They brace themselves against the wind
As it comes whistling by,
But comes the chill
Of winter-kill;
They'll tumble down and die!

The Bible states: "There is a time
To everything a season,"
I pray to die
When wild geese fly;
Just go - not ask the reason!

Elizabeth Kopp

*To every thing
there is a season,
and a time to every purpose
under the heaven...*
Eccl. 3:1

*P*raise to Thee, my Lord,
for all Your creatures…
St. Francis of Assisi

Best Remembered

We are best and long remembered -
By the people, on this earth -
For the gifts we leave behind us
That perpetuate their worth,
But our Lord is greater mindful
Of the deeds we do each day
That perpetuate His kindness
In just simple, Christian ways.

He is not impressed by gestures
Of a single gift of heart
That is meant to praise our kindness -
Even after we depart -
For it is His proven wisdom
That the measure of our worth
Is the daily, Christian duties
We perform upon this earth.

Little deeds and acts of kindness
That we choose to do each day,
To remove another's hardship
Or make light another's way;
And to share our wealth and blessings
With the needs of suffering lots -
To be longest, best remembered,
In our Lord's most Sacred Heart.

Michael Dubina

And in doing good,
let us not fail,
for in due time we shall reap,
if we do not give up.
Gala. 6:9

The Golden Years of Life

God in His loving and all-wise way
Makes the heart that once was young and gay
Serene and more gentle and less restless, too,
Content to remember the joys it once knew...
And all that we sought on "the pathway of pleasure"
Becomes but a memory to cherish and treasure -
The fast pace grows slower and the spirit serene,
And our souls can envision what our eyes have not seen...
And so while "life's springtime" is sweet to recall,
The "autumn of life" is the best time of all,
For our wild youthful yearnings all gradually cease
And God fills our days with beauty and peace!

Helen Steiner Rice

But the path of the just
is as the shining light,
that shineth more and more
unto the perfect day.
Proverbs 4:18

A Helping Hand

I wish I had the power
and could take control each day,
Of all the little habits
that I'd like to throw away.

I would wake up in the morning
and breathe the clean fresh air,
And pray for help all through the day
and know it would be there.

To never ever criticize,
would be a place to start.
I only would speak happy words,
That come straight from the heart.

Then I'd ask for patience
To last all through the day,
Then tolerance of all the folks
Who pass along my way.

I'm very sure that this would work,
if I only make the stand,
So please God, be there when I call,
and give a helping hand.

Evelene E. Henrion

Hear the sound of my cry,
my king and my God...
Ps. 5:2

Pathways

I've traveled many pathways in
The years I've spent on Earth;
Some paths have led to heartache, but
More paths have led to mirth.

Some paths were far too steep to climb,
Yet with my silent prayer,
God sent an added touch of strength
And faith to get me there.

I've flown across Pacific seas
To fair Hawaiian isles,
Then found their beauty equaled by
My children's precious smiles.

I've wandered through ripe fields of wheat
That equaled treasured gold;
I've climbed to glaciered mountain peaks,
So splendid to behold.

I've gone through valleys of despair
In shadows dark and deep,
Yet God reached down to comfort me
Whenever I would weep.

I've strolled beside a beach where whales
Cavorted happily,
Inspiring poetry in praise
Of God's great majesty!

Yes, I have traveled far and known
Both pain and happiness,
Yet found, as I look back on life,
A fact I must confess:

No matter where the paths have led,
The best one I have trod
Was when, as just a little child...
I chose the path to God!

Sandra Town Lytle

...make the way known to me
wherein I should walk,
for I have lifted up my soul to Thee.
Ps. 143:8

That Mailman
of Ours

I so can remember
Aback quite awhile,
When he brought me a letter
That made my heart smile.
I can still see him walking
His back bent from the load
But still a cheerful "Hello"
As he trudged down the road.
In the warmth of a summer
How can one forget
The beads on his forehead
His back, covered with sweat.
Gray hair and red-faced
A smile on his face
He had a cheer in his heart
That any soul could embrace.
And O' this look backwards
The past so empowers,
I remember so well...
That sweet mailman of ours.
I speak of a time when...
I... a child at play
Still... there's a warmth in my heart
For this sweet yesterday.

James Joseph Huesgen

Chain of Command

My God is first in all that I do
and as He loves me, I now love you.
To Him be the glory for all He has done
for saving my soul by sending His Son.

My family's next in my chain of command.
They share my life and it has been grand.
My wife is a blessing, a bundle of love;
my children add sunshine that comes from above.

Next are the friends who down through the years
filled me with laughter and helped dry my tears.
Some dear ones have passed; some new ones have come,
and all have stood by me tight as a drum.

My chain of command grows larger each day
as the Savior keeps sending new friends my way.
My God is first in all that I do...
the joy He gives me I offer to you!

Clay Harrison

...If we love one another,
God lives in us and
His love is perfected in us.
1 John 4:12

My Heavenly Father

My heavenly Father who dwells in love,
Thine is a kingdom of glory above.

Bestow on me please, the bread that I eat
And forgive me all of my debts complete,

As I, my debtors, try to do.
Lead me, when tempted, safely through.

Let evil, me, not assail.
Thy will be done, Thy kingdom prevail

In heaven and earth, the same.
Love is Thy immortal name.

Time without end, Thine has ever been
The kingdom and power and glory.   Amen.

Walter Kamens

…Pray then like this…
Matt. 6:9

My Choices

I don't want to live forever -
Neither do I want to die
At a time when life is pleasant
And I have no need to cry;
I would like the Lord to call me
When I'm lonely, old and grey
And I suffer from some ailment
That grows greater every day.
But - dear Lord - I beg Your patience
Not to call me in the Spring
Or in Summer time of splendors -
When the world of Nature sings.
I would choose You call in Winter -
When the world is bleak and cold
And the earth denies me comforts
From the chills of being old.

Michael Dubina

Little
Country Church

While riding in the country
Amid the rolling hills,
I saw a little country church,
Oh, I can see it still!

Although no sound of pealing,
There must have been a bell,
Because I saw a steeple small
From which I heard no knell.

The little church was weathered,
This I could clearly see,
But yet it mattered not at all
For it was dear to me!

Tho' years are swiftly passing,
Which bring both joy and pain,
That little church in memory
Remains a sweet refrain!

Sancie Earman King

Reason to Praise

You give me reason to praise You, Lord,
With every breath I take -
For only You make possible
Every move I make.

Each happy little blessing
That ever comes my way
Is never a coincidence,
But You Who lights the way.

And when I'm sad and feel alone
And no one understands,
You're always there when I reach up,
To gladly take my hand.

Oh, what comfort and joy to know
I have a Friend so true!
Lord, every time I seek Your will,
You show me what to do.

So hear my praise I offer You
- It's bursting from my heart -
For each new day I walk with You,
Just makes more praises start!

Denise A. DeWald

*"I will extol
the Lord at all times;
His praise will always
be on my lips."*
Psalm 34:1

They who sow in tears
shall reap in joy.
Ps. 126:5

Seasons
of the Heart

The heart has many seasons,
Just as this good old earth,
And they all combine together,
To comprise what we are worth.
There is a childhood innocence,
In which we dream and play,
There is a time for growing up,
And making our own way.

There is a time for keeping,
And a time for letting go,
A time for moving swiftly,
And a time for walking slow.
There is a time for learning,
And a time for teaching, too,
And there is time for resting,
When all the chores are through.

We all know joy and sorrow,
'Tis written in the plan,
But Heaven waits beyond life's gates,
For every earnest man.
Each life has many pictures,
And all a work of art,
But what a silver symphony,
...The seasons of the heart.

Grace E. Easley

My Father, the King

The lilies of the field
Rejoice in His light.
The stars in the heavens
Exalt Him by night.
And I, how may I show
The wonder I feel?
The pleasures I know
As I reverently kneel
Before my Father, the King?

The earth's mighty mountains
Exult in His ways.
The forest giants lift up
Their branches in praise.
And I, how may I proclaim
His eternal glory?
The power in His name -
The unending story
Of my Father, the King?

Gloria Patri
The mockingbird sings.
The earth shouts hosannas
To the King of all kings.
And I, how may I present
My offering of love
For each blessing that's sent
From the storehouse above
By my eternal Father, the King?

William Daniel Robinson

Restoration

All things in life that I have earned
and everything I own,
Results from the work I've done
but I was not alone.
Without His strength to comfort me,
without His loving care,
I'd not have made it thru the days
of deep and dark despair.

With gentle hands He lifted me
when I was feeling low;
His mighty power touched my soul
and eased my pain and woe.
So now the work I do each day
I offer to the Lord.
With heartfelt gratitude I've found
my faith has been restored.

Angie Monnens

Come to me,
all you who are weary
and burdened,
and I will give you rest.
Matt. 11:28

Jade

Summer is jade growing everywhere,
Like an undiscovered prayer,
God smiles upon the world with green,
And paints a picture postcard scene.

The rivers, too, have turned to jade,
The hills, the grass, so newly made,
The leaves that dance in their bright lace,
Wearing a happy summer face.

I thank God for all colors He
Makes from His rainbows just for me,
Of all the ones that He has made
Most of all, I love His jade!

Marion Schoeberlein

He has made
everything beautiful
in its time...
Eccl. 3:11

If, Because of My Life...

When my race is run -
If I've left but one
Whose life was touched by mine,
Will be worth it all -
At that final call,
To hear, "Child, you did fine."

If one soul was saved -
From a fiery grave,
Because of God's mercy I told,
Life was not spent in vain -
For I'll meet with my gain
When Heaven, at last, I behold.

If by something I've done -
God a vic'try has won,
Then my life's been especially blessed.
I can leave here knowing -
He reaped seeds I've been sowing,
And I've earned my eternal rest.

Diana Sue Helmer

The Simple Things in Life...

...Each morning fresh with crystal dew
And sunlight on my face
The pitter-patter of the rain
And children's table grace.
...The softness of a baby's cheek
A little hand in mine
The fragrance of magnolia trees
Or honeysuckle vines.
...A table laden with good food
And loved ones gathered near
Those simple blessings from our God
So special, oh so dear.
...The sound of music that I love
The song a robin sings,
That joy inside the heart of man
Where hope eternal springs.
...The moonlight beaming on the earth
The sounds of night I hear
A hush that rests the weary heart
God's presence oh so near.
...The precious little gifts of love
God gives to us each day
Those simple blessings from above
To brighten up our way.

Gertrude B. McClain

Blessed are they
that fear the Lord...
you will eat the fruit of your labor...
and it shall be well with you.
Ps. 128:1-2

Day of
Pleasures

This has been a day of pleasures -
Doing service to the Lord
And enjoying all His blessings
Of affection and reward.
I have fed a hungry beggar
And made light a stranger's load -
By each place, where paths were tangled,
I have marked the Christian road;
And I've taken time from labor
To assist a friend in need -
From the bounties of my harvests,
I have given neighbors seed
But it's, now, my time to worship -
And to thank Him for the ways
He had multiplied my pleasures
For each love I gave away.

Michael Dubina

Bear ye
one another's burdens,
and so you will fulfil
the law of Christ.
Gala. 6:2

Count

Count the grains of sand upon a beach
Or the raindrops in a storm,
Count the sunbeams as they dance about
So comforting and warm.
Count each and every twinkling star
Up in the heaven so blue,
The count is small compared to love
Our Savior has for you.

Count the leaves on every tree
And the birds that rest therein,
Count the ants in every hill
And all the fish that swim.
The count would be so large I fear
It never could be told,
But small compared to love we get
From the Savior of our soul.

Albert N. Theel

Along the Shore

I love to walk along the shore,
For there is peace, and evermore,
I walk with arms outstretched to Thee,
For You made all of this for me.

Of rocks I search for beauty there -
They hide from me, I know not where.
And still occasionally I find,
A rock unlike among its kind.

There's beauty there upon the shore
Not only rocks, but so much more.
There's beauty in the scenery,
Of windswept beach, and I am free.

I'm free from woes of city life.
I'm free from hate and free from strife.
While walking on the beach with Thee,
Somehow my soul at last is free!

Clayton G. Moseley

Best Friend

The Lord is my refuge
My Haven of "Rest,"
He shields and protects me
When faced with "Life's Tests."
I go to Him always in prayer for release,
He never forsakes me
But gives me His "Peace."
I fret not - nor worry
Burdens are laid at His feet -
I trust and obey Him
Whenever we meet!
Be happy - not fretful
Be glad and not sad,
The Lord is my "Keeper"
The "Best Friend" I have!

Kathryn Wiesenhoefer

*And call upon Me
in the day of trouble:
I will deliver thee
and thou shalt glorify Me.*
Ps. 50:15

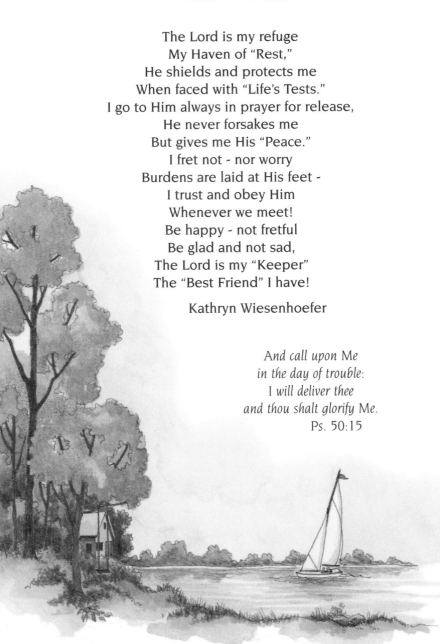

I Have a Friend
That's Dear to Me

I have a friend that's dear to me
Who's never heard of Calvary -
Who doesn't know about God's power
Or strength that's there for every hour!

Who has no song within the heart
The Holy Spirit can impart.
Who's not enjoyed the peace you find -
As God quiets a troubled mind!

Or felt the lightening of one's load
While traveling down life's weary road.
Nor found the pleasure of sin's diversion,
We seek and find upon conversion!

My friend imagines I'm deprived -
But, O! The blessings I've derived!
It's pretty selfish! Just not fair!
To have all this and never share!

Verle Elizabeth Davis

The Lord
is compassionate
and merciful, slow to anger
and abounding in love.
Ps. 103:8

Together
Again

Somewhere there's a place
Where our little friends go,
And they wait for us there
'Cause... they love us so.

But here on this earth
We hear no woof, or no mew,
But there's a happier place
And they wait there for you.

They will tumble and roll
And jump in the air,
When the day comes
You, too, will be there.

Reunited once more
In this wonderful place,
Where your tears and your sadness
Will all be erased.

James Joseph Huesgen

Our Book
of Life

Our book of life holds pages rare
For all the words we're writing there,
Each moment that we spend on earth
It all begins at time of birth,
The times of joy - the times of strife
Until the very end of life.

Life is a book God grants to each
To find the dreams within our reach,
The smiles and tears - the moments bright
And every blessing in our sight,
Sometimes we fail, though oft' succeed
Life grants the courage that we need.

Record each page with loving care
And live each day in hope and prayer,
No moment spent can then return
No matter how your heart might yearn,
A page anew each day we write
Recorded in our book of life.

Garnett Ann Schultz

April
Showers

God whispers to each living plant
And wakes each bulb to flower,
With gentle rain that comes in Spring,
We call an April shower.

He sends the sun to warm the earth
And grass begins to grow,
Then little buds form on the trees
Because He loves us so.

Though Winter storms may come and go
With icy winds that blow,
Plants wait for Him as though asleep
Beneath the drifting snow.

Just as the bulbs and grass and trees
Burst forth in one accord,
I, too, must learn to weather storms
And wait upon the Lord.

Ruth Moloney Cowgill

Every Day's Worth Living!

Sometimes we need to be alone;
sometimes we need a friend.
Sometimes we pray throughout the night
for broken hearts to mend.

We sometimes pray for miracles,
but miss them when they come.
In our search for long-stemmed roses,
we overlook the mums!

God sometimes sends us showers,
and often we complain,
But there would be no rainbows
if never there was rain!

This world is ever changing;
each day brings something new,
And we're old before we know it
with much we'd like to do.

Each day God sends us blessings
that we may overlook,
But every day's worth living
when we live it by His Book!

Clay Harrison

I need some quiet time with God,
To help me through the day:
A little time to read His word,
A little time to pray.
From this I gain the strength I need
To carry me along;
It lifts me up on wings of joy
And gives my heart a song.

Sandra Town Lytle

All That's Beautiful

For all that's beautiful dear Lord
I thank You oh so much,
The blue skies and a field of flowers
The raindrop's gentle touch.
The tall trees reaching for the sky
The birds that soar so high,
The moonlight as it touches earth
The stars there in the sky.
The music that is sweeter than
A thousand words could tell,
The snowfall on a winter night
The ocean's mighty swell.
A little baby's innocence
The children as they play
They are so beautiful to see
In such a special way.

For all that's beautiful dear Lord
The things that we can't see,
The beauty of a brand-new love
As magic as can be.
Or years of love and laughter
Then wrinkles on the brow,
But love shines ever youthful
With memories of those vows.
This world has so much beauty
A gift from God above,
But most of all the beauty
Of God's own changeless love.

Gertrude B. McClain

Dawn and Dusk

If you deny there is a God
Or if you walk in doubt,
Just let your eyes behold the skies
And take a look about.
Consider, now, the dawn and dusk,
The brightness of the day,
And how the darkness settles when
The sun has slipped away.
Consider just these miracles,
The morning and the night,
The fear in every shadow and
The hope in every light.
Oh, there are other miracles
Including life and death,
As earthly science cannot find
The origin of breath.
But just behold the changing sky
And ask yourself again,
If there is not a God, Who is
The Ruler of all men?

James J. Metcalfe

On a Day So Fair

On an Autumn day so fair
While strolling lazily,
Sights and smells of nature fill
My heart with untold glee.

Pink and white chrysanthemums
Nod lightly in the breeze,
A stand of sweet, red clover wafts
Its perfume through the trees.

Fields of yellow asters sway
Like waves at eventide,
Mint leaves spread their fragrances
All through the countryside.

As I watch the sun go down
Along the river banks,
I revel in God's wonders, and
I say a prayer of thanks.

Angie Monnens

My Trust

Sometimes, I find it hard to pray.
I stumble thru a troubled day
And feeling hurt and sad of heart,
Self-pity stirs and plays its part
To foster thoughts and doubts, I know,
I must not nurture nor let grow.

For if I close my mind to You
My eyes will lock on earth's sad view.
And so I plead, Lord, help me see
How much Your love can mean to me.
Just let me cling to Your strong hands
And help me tread earth's shifting sands.

Helen M. Motti

When I am afraid,
I put my trust in You.
In God, whose word I praise,
I trust without a fear...
Ps. 56:3, 4

I Believe
in Miracles

I believe in miracles
I see them every day,
Where grass springs fresh and green,
Where bright-eyed children play.

So many miracles I view
I need no greater proof,
A tulip blooming on my sill,
Blue sky above my roof.

From out my window I can see
A robin build his nest,
Each day in countless little ways
With miracles I'm blessed.

And when my heart is lonely
God sends a friend my way,
I believe in miracles
I see them every day!

Kay Hoffman

*...Great and wonderful
are your works,
Lord God Almighty:
just and true are thy ways,
O King of Ages.
Rev. 15:3*

Needing You

I needed You - how much I needed You
And never once thought it be true
So close at hand - You'd always be
To lift me up and set me free!
I felt in bondage - every turn
You taught me much I had to learn
Through years of struggling and the strife,
That this was part of living life.
You're always near to pick me up
When drinking from the "bitter cup" -
To lean on You at every hour
And feel the strength of Your great power.
You taught me what I had to know
From this "weak" heart
You'll never go!

Kathryn Wiesenhoefer

For I reckon that the sufferings
of the present time are not worthy
to be compared with the glory to come,
that shall be revealed in us.
Romans 8:18

Smiles

Smiles are the precious gems
that add a special glow,
And fill the world with sunshine
in spite of daily woe.
Smiles are the soft, white clouds
that cushion every blow;
And chase away misgivings
among our friends and foe.
Smiles are the rainbows that
appear when storms are through;
They turn our pain to joy again -
our courage we'll renew.
Smiles are the bridge between
the darkness and the light;
When sharing them with others,
new friendships we invite.

Angie Monnens

Believe

Do you doubt that God is present,
When the sun sets in the west -
While you stand upon a hilltop
When He puts the earth to rest,
While the clouds turn red and yellow
Underneath an azure sky,
And the wind in all the pine trees,
Whispers softly a lullaby?

Do you doubt a greater power
Holds your life within His hand -
Can't you sense a Supreme Being,
Where the ocean meets the land?

Do you sense a better purpose
In your life sent from above,
Than the petty quarrels of mankind,
When so many need your love?

Do you doubt that Christ lived on this earth,
Two thousand years ago,
To lead us in His sacred steps
So that all the world would know,
The Lord died for our sins upon a cross
And in His loving grace,
All who believe shall live with Him,
In Heaven's eternal place.

A. Eugene Koons

Cloud
Shepherd

Across the sky, a gusty wind
is driving flocks of clouds.
They move along like herds of sheep,
in bunchy, trotting crowds
And here and there you see,
like small lambs left behind,
Small clouds the wind comes herding
in, a shepherd, good and kind.
They hurry fast to catch the flock
of grey old ewes ahead
Until, down cross the western sky,
where sun glows warm and red,
The shepherd wind does herd them
home to shelter in the hills.
It's then he rests, along with
them. His herding whistle stills
And peace flows o'er the meadow
sky, with daisy stars alight,
As sheep and shepherd, wind and
cloud began a peaceful night.

Minnie Boyd Popish

I will lay down
in peace and sleep,
for the Lord protects me.
Ps. 4:8

Blessings

Let's count our blessings one by one
As through this life we go,
We may find out that we are blessed
Much more than ere we know.

First of all we're blessed with life,
Next I'm sure comes health,
Then if we truly seek the way
God blesses us with wealth.

Not of a monetary kind
Tho' that is nice I'm sure,
But wealth in our dear Savior's love
To cleanse and keep us pure.

All through our life these blessings
Will flow down from above,
Anointed by our Savior's grace
And His undying love.

Albert N. Theel

*The Lord
hath been
mindful of us,
and hath
blessed us...*
Ps. 115:12

A Traitor Within

Sometimes I have a wonderful faith
That takes trouble on the chin -
But then again, there's fear inside,
For a traitor lies within!

Yes, in my inner self there lies
A traitor to my trust:
And that's a fear-filled heart within
Oft' crumbles faith to dust!

Praise God, that in my weakness,
He strengthens against that thief -
When I cry to Him, "I do believe!
Help Thou my unbelief!"

Lynn Fenimore Nuzzi

*And straightway
the father cried out,
and said with tears,
"Lord, I believe;
help Thou mine unbelief."*
Mark 9:24

Prayer

Grant that I may see no evil,
In the neighbor at my side,
Lord, that I may speak no evil,
Through intent or foolish pride.
So my ears may hear no evil,
Let Thy voice be raised above
Everyday distractions, so that
I may grow in faith and love.

You have promised to be with me,
You have said "be not afraid,"
You are ready to forgive me
Each mistake that I have made,
Loving me too much to grant me
Everything for which I've prayed.

Grace E. Easley

Winter,
and God Cares

Once again the earth is bare.
The sky is gray.
The wind is cold.
The cattle on the hillside flee
before the storm.
The sheep are safe within
the shepherd's fold.

God speaks through every season,
for He cares for all His own -
The sparrow hiding in the eaves,
seeds lying fallow in the ground,
Squirrels snug within their nests,
Bears in caves and frogs in ponds,
Human beings o'er all the earth,
Even stars up in the sky.
Yes, even though it's winter's dearth,
God is ever nigh.

Maridee Cook

Song for
a Stormy Day

When summer winds turn harsh and cold
with wild and angry cries,
and withered autumn leaves are swept
into the frosted skies
so that our hearts feel faint and weak
and we feel forced to yield -
reach for the strengthening of love
and let it be your shield.

As bitterness of winter storms
becomes a sunwarmed breeze,
we, too, can let love's gentleness
transform our agonies.
Like spring that whispers in the rain
and scents the earth with flowers
Hope offers promises of faith
and rainbows for dark hours.

Eugene G. E. Botelho

Before the Dawn Tomorrow

My friend, don't take for granted
the things you have today,
For before the dawn tomorrow
they could be taken away.
God provides for those who trust Him
and meets each basic need,
But never has He promised
to satisfy our need.

Have you shared the things He gave you
with someone who had less,
Or been a friend to those in need
while asking God to bless?
Have you praised the One who feeds you
and gives you daily bread,
And you have enough left over
for others to be fed?

Have you thanked Him for strength to do
each job that must be done...
Or did you accept the glory
never thanking anyone?
My friend, don't take for granted
the things you have today,
For you could become the beggar
you scolded yesterday!

Clay Harrison

My Wealth

How rich I am in ever faithful friends,
Unchanging as the seasons come and go,
In my love for beauty, which I find
Is everywhere, in everything I know.
How precious is the time I have been given,
To appreciate all God has made,
A humble heart, forever giving thanks
Because of that for which He dearly paid.

How rich I am, no fortune can compare
To all that I possess within my soul,
Come what may, in spite of banks which fail,
These gifts are mine to always have and hold.
The interest which I earn does far surpass
The highest rate that's offered anywhere,
Because I am not earning gold, but God,
...And thus my wealth remains beyond compare.

Grace E. Easley

*But seek ye first
the Kingdom of God...*
Luke 12:31

Perfect
Little Snowflakes

Perfect little snowflakes dancing through the air,
Messengers of winter ever soft and fair,
Lighting on the streamlet quickly melt away,
Adding wondrous beauty to a winter day.

Perfect little snowflakes silent as they fall,
Bits of icy magic loved by one and all,
Dressing naked branches piling thick and deep,
Over field and meadow all the world asleep.

Laughing little children sledding on the hill,
Cheeks all bright and rosy fondest dreams fulfill,
Catching winter magic, hearts all bright and gay,
Perfect little snowflakes, lovely winter day.

Garnett Ann Schultz

The Wonderment of Snow!

When I was just a little girl,
Excited I would grow;
When I could watch, through windowpanes,
Descent of fleecy snow!
For even to this very day,
I recall what Mother said;
That when the snow was deep enough,
I could get out my sled!
And oh what special joy to me,
Was sledding down a hill;
At time there was no traffic jam,
So all was sweet and still!
And most of all, at Christmastime,
Was snow a wondrous sight;
As it descended from the sky,
So Christmas would be white!
But now that I have older grown,
And thus can sled no more;
I still can watch, through windowpanes,
The snow, which just restores!
But most important thing of all,
Tho' not one flake I see;
I thank my God for childhood days
When snow brought joy to me!

Sancie Earman King

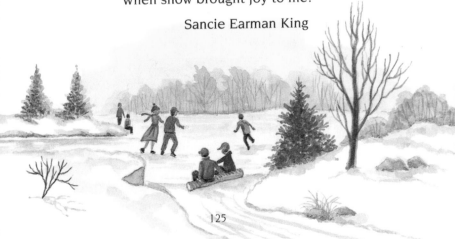

New Hope

How deep is the darkness,
how long is the night
for a soul in despair,
in search of the light?
How many a heartache,
how many a sigh,
who counts all the teardrops
which fall by and by?

How great the rejoicing,
how sweet the delight
when darkness surrenders
to soft morning light.
New hope is ascending
on wings of the morn,
from yesterday's sorrows
new dreams have been born.

Regina Wiencek

Trust in Him

You may trust our Lord and Saviour
To be Shepherd of your life
If your faith, in Him, is constant
In your trials of grief and strife
For, in times of tears and struggle,
We are tempted into sins
That are comforts - for the moment -
But deny our trust in Him.

Be, forever, true and faithful -
With a Christian faith of heart
That is never worn or lessened
By the doubts that trials impart;
He will comfort and sustain you -
On this earth and up above -
If you trust Him with conviction
And devotion of your love.

Michael Dubina

The All-Wise God

I wonder where the morning goes
When afternoon arrives;
I wonder if it has a spot
Where it can quietly hide.
And where does afternoon time go
When twilight shadows fall?
I wonder if it waits somewhere
Till it's again on call.
To where do twilight shadows steal
When night shades dot the scene?
I wonder if they dissipate
Into a tranquil dream.
Too, where is nighttime's rendezvous
When morning gilds the skies?
Man stands in awe, a-wondering,
But God knows; He's all-wise.

Loise Pinkerton Fritz

To the only wise God our Saviour,
be glory and majesty, dominion and power,
both now and ever. Amen.
Jude - Verse 25